The Nadder Valley

IN OLD PHOTOGRAPHS

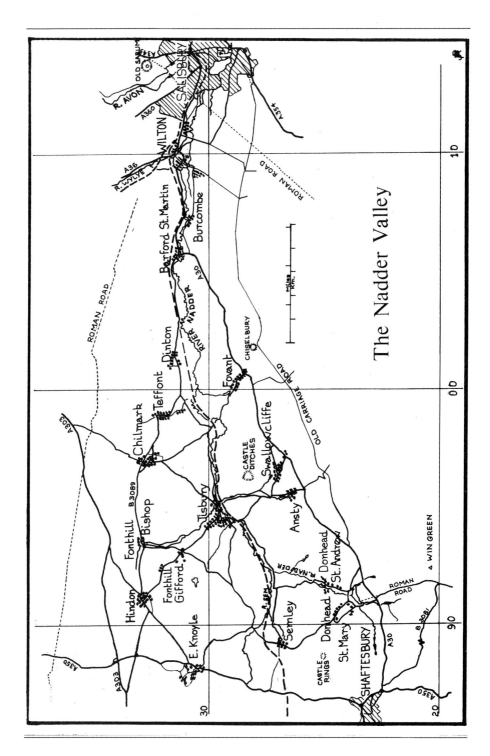

The Nadder Valley

The Nadder Valley

IN OLD PHOTOGRAPHS

REX SAWYER

Alan Sutton Publishing Limited
Phoenix Mill · Far Thrupp · Stroud
Gloucestershire

First Published 1994

British Library Cataloguing in Publication Data.
A catalogue record for this book is available from
the British Library.

ISBN 0-7509-0811-4

Typeset in 9/10 Sabon.
Typesetting and origination by
Alan Sutton Publishing Limited.
Printed in Great Britain by
Hartnolls, Bodmin, Cornwall.

Wilton House, the home of the Earls of Pembroke since Tudor times. In 1647, the Elizabethan mansion was destroyed by fire and the present one was built by Inigo Jones and his nephew, John Webb. As principal landowners, patrons and employers the Pembrokes have continued to influence Wilton and its surrounding area. (Chris Rousell)

Contents

Introduction

Rising in the chalk hills to the east of Shaftesbury, the River Nadder begins its tortuous route through some of the most beautiful pastoral country in south Wiltshire. Fed by springs from the Donheads, the Nadder links with the River Sem north of Wardour before continuing its leisurely course through such historic settlements as Tisbury, Dinton and Wilton, the ancient capital of Wessex. At Quidhampton it merges with the Wylye to join the Avon at Salisbury and continues its final journey to the sea at Christchurch.

Its name, literally 'winding water', is believed to derive from the Celtic words *nydd*, to twist or wind, and *dwr* meaning water. The Saxons called it 'naedre' meaning a serpent. Both aptly describe a waterway whose meandering course adds so much to the variety of the landscape through which it passes.

Beloved of fishermen, walkers and environmentalists alike, the Nadder Valley has not suffered the over-exposure of tourism. Although possessing magnificent country houses and vistas of great beauty, its charm lies in the secretive bends of the river and its rich diversity of scenery. Woods, fields, narrow waterways and gently undulating hills – these are the backcloth to the hamlets and twisting country lanes that so bewilder the explorer.

This book, a companion to the author's forthcoming *A Wiltshire Valley – Tales of the Nadder*, looks at the villages that have formed within its watershed. In photographs mostly dating from the beginning of the 20th century, it documents a rural society now largely transformed. It should be pointed out that the comparatively small number of photographs depicting some villages is due to the scarcity of material available rather than any attempt to devalue their importance. Similarly, the relatively short section on Wilton does not reflect its true economic and social influence on the valley. This has already been depicted admirably in Peter Daniels' *Around Wilton in Old Photographs* (Alan Sutton, 1991). I have merely tried to 'fill out' a little the picture he has presented.

My thanks for so much valuable assistance must go to the many inhabitants of the Nadder Valley and beyond who have preserved and kindly loaned the photographs shown here. This includes the various branches of the Women's Institute which initiated a Village Scrapbook Competition in the 1950s and thereby preserved so much that would otherwise have been lost. The same must be said of those who created the Archives Rooms at Tisbury and Hindon. Their efforts have also preserved much of historical value and provided centres of study for those who wish to learn more about the Nadder Valley. Neither

Fishing on the Nadder early this century. (Dinton WI Scrapbook, 1956)

must I forget the original photographers, many anonymous, whose efforts in the past have provided these insights. The staff of Salisbury Local Studies Library and many Nadder Valley friends have assisted my researches in identifying the people, places and events depicted here. Most of all, I must record my gratitude to Rex Galpin who has spent many hours reproducing the prints in this book.

SECTION ONE

The Donheads

The sheepwash at Ludwell, Donhead St Mary, around the time of the First World War.
(Donheads WI Scrapbook, 1956)

Donhead Hall and Deer Park. A handsome Grade II listed building of the early Georgian period. It was once the home of the illegitimate son of Sir Godfrey Kneller, famous Dutch painter of the courts of William of Orange and George I. (Donheads WI Scrapbook)

Jerry Sanger, market gardener from the Coombes, Donhead St Mary, at the end of the 19th century. He hated having his photograph taken, hence the look of surprise! (Fred Peckham)

Schoolchildren at Donhead St Mary Board School, 1885. (Fred Peckham)

William Arnold, founder of a market-gardening business at Church Hill, Donhead St Mary, in the latter half of the 19th century. (Fred Peckham)

The will of Sarah Ann Burt, 1904. Thomas and Sarah Ann Burt farmed at Watery Lane Farm, Donhead St Mary, at the end of the nineteenth century. (Agnes Penny)

Percy, Cissie and Annie Goddard at Watery Lane Farm, the home of their maternal grandparents, Thomas and Sarah Ann Burt. Their mother, Elizabeth Burt, had married Henry Goddard and moved to a smaller farm near Crewkerne. The Burt family moved to Guy's Marsh in the 1890s. (Fred Peckham)

'Aunt Jane's Cottage', Donhead St Mary, from a painting by Kathleen Blanchard, 1920s. Situated near Church Hill, it has now been demolished. (Fred Peckham)

Donhead House was previously the vicarage of Donhead St Andrew. The last vicar to live there, Horace Chapman, converted to Roman Catholicism, and enlarged the house in 1895. (Donheads WI Scrapbook)

The Carpenter's Arms, Donhead St Andrew. This closed in the mid-1950s, and the last landlord was Alfie Ingram. (Donheads WI Scrapbook)

This cartoon depicts Shaftesbury Fire Brigade arriving four hours after being called to a fire at Whitesands Cross, Donhead St Andrew, in the 1920s. The artist was Mr Wilmot, the Shaftesbury chimney sweep. (Vi Head)

Ferne House, Donhead St Andrew. From 1563 it was the home of the Grove family. The medieval house was replaced by this one in 1811 which was in turn demolished in 1964. From 1915 it was the home of the Duke and Duchess of Hamilton and Brandon and remained so until the duchess's death in 1951. (Donheads WI Scrapbook)

This photograph shows a group of dogs leaving London for the animal refuge at Ferne House. It was run by Nina, the Duchess of Hamilton and Brandon, during and after the Second World War, and the animals were all refugees from blitzed homes. (Vi Head)

SECTION TWO
Semley

Attempts to enclose the common land around Semley have always been fiercely resisted. Until the mid-20th century there were gates across the village lanes to prevent animals from straying. Increasing traffic led to their removal and animals no longer graze on the unfenced areas. (Semley WI Scrapbook, 1956)

The old Poor House at Sem Hill, which is now a private residence. (Semley WI Scrapbook)

Semley station, 1911. A small industrial centre and a hotel developed around this station which was closed in the mid-1960s. (Joyce Johnson)

The United Dairies depot at Semley station, seen here around the time of the First World War, when solid tyre vehicles and 17-gallon churns were still being used. Bert Woodrow, the driver, is standing by his open-sided cab. (Semley WI Scrapbook)

The United Dairies depot and manager's house at Semley station, between the wars. Also visible is the latest state-of-the-art milk pipeline which linked directly to specially designed tankers on the railway sidings. (Semley WI Scrapbook)

Taken in the 1920s, before their marriage, this photograph shows William Mallett and Sally Dewey, publicans at the Railway Hotel. The pub is now known as the Kingsettle. (Louisa George)

Workmen at Knipe Farm, Gutch Common, 1932. On the horse is George Stone, son of Ebenezer, the local carrier, whose legs were blown off during the First World War. (Joyce Johnson)

A popular village meeting point: outside the Benett Arms, 1910. (Joyce Johnson)

William Sully, the blacksmith, who died in 1965. His wrought ironwork can still be seen in many Semley gates and in the seat on Calais Hill. (Semley WI Scrapbook)

Semley Home Guard practising with a selection of weapons at Gutch Common during the Second World War. Jim Hall is in the centre of the back row. Is that a German spy in the background? (David Ricketts)

Children dressed for the May Festival, c. 1918. Second from the left is Ida Toogood of Gutch Common; Florrie Haynes is eighth from the left. (David Ricketts)

Workers at Kirton Farm, pictured earlier this century. Left to right: Lisle Brice (the farmer), ? Dibben, Ray Gumm, Bill Toogood, Gordon Hunt, -?-, Fred Ricketts, -?-. (David Ricketts)

The village outing to Southsea, 1939. The photograph includes Mrs Guy, Mrs Penny, Mrs Beaton, Mrs Judd, Mrs Coward, Mrs Jones, Mrs Pyart, Mrs Ellis, Miss Judd, Mrs Ricketts, Maureen Pitart, Mrs Pitman, Miss Jay, Mrs Coward jr and children, Miss Phylis Sharples and Mary Garrett. (David Ricketts)

Semley WI group at Thanes, 1939. Back row, left to right: Mrs Beaton, Mrs Jones, Mrs Fitzmaurice, Mrs W.G. Pitman, Miss Rays, Mrs Rays, Miss Nutbeam, Miss A. Jay, Miss Phylis Sharples (president), Mrs Young, Miss Burden, Miss Haines, Mrs Ricketts, Mrs Penny. Seated: Mrs Ellis, Mrs Coward, Mrs Coward jr (and three little Cowards), Mrs Judd, Miss Bennett and Twinkles, the Cairn terrier. (Semley WI Scrapbook, 1956)

SECTION THREE

Hindon

A tea party at Hindon early this century. Pictured, left to right, are Mrs Vic Read, Mrs J. Ranger and Mrs G. Cheverall. (Hindon Village Hall Archives – VHA)

A 16th-century chapel-of-ease, *c.* 1869. This was replaced by the present church in 1870. Next to it, to the right, is the home of Charles Snook and Sons, 'plumbers, glaziers, painters and paper hangers', which was also demolished. The shop next on the right is the present post office and store, previously the Crown Inn. (Hindon VHA)

The Dean at the bottom of Hindon's main street, pictured before the First World War. It is fed by many springs and frequently flooded. (Hindon VHA)

The Reading Room had been the Petty Sessions Hall from 1867 to 1889, when it transferred from the Lamb Inn. It is now the village hall. Next to it until 1889 was the police station, where the superintendent had also lived, while two constables occupied adjacent cottages. Alongside were the police cells of which only the wall remains. From 1889, when law enforcement transferred to Tisbury, the principal smith, Mr B. Coombs, had his premises here. (Hindon VHA)

John Beckett was the Hindon basket-maker and parish clerk in the second half of the 19th century. His wife's relatives are seen selling his produce, probably in Somerset. (Hindon VHA)

Hindon High Street, 1904. The trees were planted in 1863 by Sir Michael Shaw-Stewart to commemorate the wedding of the Prince of Wales (later Edward VII). (Hindon VHA)

Hindon High Street, 1909, showing cottages above the church. Included in the picture are J. Beckett, Mrs M. Gray, Mrs Newberry and Miss Stanton. (Hindon VHA)

Hindon Band, *c*. 1920. Back row, left to right: Bill White, Albert Small, Alf Lamb, John Snook, Alfred Burgess, Henry Small, Albert Stevens, Bert Cheverell. Middle row: Bill Phillips, R. Andrews, Will Case, Jack Snook, Alban Lamb, W. Fry, Phil Smith. Front row: Walter Stevens, Charlie Smith. (Hindon VHA)

Hindon Flower Show group, 1920s. The photograph includes Mr Mills, Mr Phillips, Mr Gray, Mr Hayter, Mr Coombs, Rev. Mr Lumsden, Miss Pat Rawlings, Mrs Warren and Mr A. Lamb. (Hindon VHA)

Hindon Flower Show, *c.* 1926. The rather large committee includes William Beckett, Mr Few, Jim Warren, Ernest White, Rev. Mr Lumsden, Carl Bevis, Albert Lamb, Sid Gray, Mr Pyart, Bert Baker, Brian Coombs and Mr Mills. (Hindon VHA)

Boys enjoying (enduring?) a gardening lesson outside the schoolhouse earlier this century. (Hindon VHA)

Hindon schoolchildren, *c.* 1930, with their schoolmistress, Miss V. Andrews. (Hindon VHA)

James Knowles, the butcher, is seen outside his shop with his children, Len and Cathie, in 1913. (Hindon VHA)

Harvest time at Hindon, 1938. (Hindon VHA)

SECTION FOUR
The Fonthills

Fonthill Park. This magnificent archway is believed to have been built by Alderman William Beckford at the same time as his new residence, Fonthill Splendens, in the mid-18th century. (G.P. Wencki)

The Pavilion, *c*. 1900. Fonthill Park has been the home of many mansions. This was the remaining part of Alderman Beckford's Fonthill Splendens. The rest had been demolished by his son William to build his famous abbey. The Pavilion was the home of the Morrison family who had it demolished in 1922. (Fonthills WI Scrapbook, 1956)

James Wyatt's model of the abbey at Fonthill, which he built for William Beckford. The abbey was completed in 1800 but it had faulty foundations, and in December 1825 the tower collapsed, destroying much of the building. Today only a fragment remains. (Tisbury Archives)

Fonthill's second abbey, which was built by the Marquess of Westminster in Scottish-baronial style, south of the Beckford Abbey ruins. In 1879, after the marquess' death, his daughter, Lady Octavia, and her husband, Sir Michael Shaw-Stewart, moved into the abbey. After the Second World War its structure was found to be faulty and it was blown up in 1955, to the alarm of local villagers who thought the war had started again! (Joyce Jenkyns)

Little Ridge was the home of the Morrison family before they moved to the Pavilion. The wing on the right had been a derelict manor house and was transferred stone by stone from Berwick St Leonard by Hugh Morrison. Considered too large and rambling, the whole building was replaced by the present house at Little Ridge in 1972. (Fonthills WI Scrapbook)

Sheep on the Fonthill Downs, pictured early this century near the present A303 road. (Kathleen Mould)

The Rev. Norwood Perkins, rector of Fonthill Bishop, 1900–14. He is seen here outside the rectory, c. 1901. (Fonthills WI Scrapbook)

Thomas Coombs and his niece, Miss Applin. Thomas was churchwarden at Fonthill Bishop from 1887 to 1893, and Miss Applin was churchwarden at Berwick St Leonard from 1921 to 1946. (Fonthills WI Scrapbook)

Fonthill Bishop at the beginning of the century. The schoolchildren are standing across what is now the busy Barford to Hindon road. (Reg Harris)

A village outing from Fonthill Bishop, *c.* 1919. Note the solid tyres on the bus. The vicar is the Rev. Richard Wilton Sutcliffe. (Fonthills WI Scrapbook)

Fonthill Bishop Football Club, 1926. Back row, from left to right: Charlie Lever, Jack Hacker, Ed Newbury, Arthur Gray, -?-. Middle row: Lot Newbury, Archie Godwin, Len Priddle, Fred Churchill, Tom Newbury, Bill Dixon. Front row: Hughy Gray, Dan Conelly, Bill Ranger, Walt Samways. (Reg Harris)

Haymaking at Fonthill Park early this century. (Fonthills WI Scrapbook)

The Waterfall at the southern end of Fonthill Lake as it was until its redevelopment a few years ago. This photograph was taken in 1905. (Pamela Bown)

One of the lodges at the southern entrance to Fonthill Park at the beginning of the century. The lodges were designed by George Devey, a Victorian architect. (Reg Harris)

The old sawmills at Fonthill Gifford, pictured during the First World War. (Fonthills WI Scrapbook)

Workers at the Fonthill Gifford sawmills during the First World War. (Fonthills WI Scrapbook)

A cottage in Stop Street, Fonthill Gifford, before the First World War. (Fonthills WI Scrapbook)

The village outing from Fonthill Gifford, *c.* 1925. (Fonthills WI Scrapbook)

SECTION FIVE

Tisbury

Election Day. The scene is Tisbury Square, probably in 1900, when J.A. Morrison of Fonthill Park was returned as Member of Parliament. George Ponton (holding the horse's head) is standing outside his shop. The Pontons were saddlers, and their business was established in 1865. The shop is now a hairdresser's. (Kathleen Mould)

This is the view from Chantry Hill above the station and looking across Tisbury in the 1900s. The gasholder in the foreground was removed in 1921. (Kathleen Mould)

The bridge over the Nadder at Tisbury, photographed early this century. The Salisbury, Semley and Gillingham Dairies Depot is on the left and the new Roman Catholic church is on the right. (Joyce Jenkyns)

A cricket match at the end of the 19th century. Behind it can be seen the line of small trees where The Avenue now stands (constructed in 1881). Beyond is Zion Hill Chapel, sited on the present Park Road. (Kathleen Mould)

The River Nadder in flood, with Tisbury Church in the background. The magnitude of the deluge suggests that this photograph was taken in 1910, when the nave of Salisbury Cathedral was flooded. (Tisbury Archives – the late Mrs A. Galpin)

The return of the bells to Tisbury Parish Church after their restoration, 1926. (Tisbury Archives – the late Mrs A. Galpin)

A confirmation service, taken by Bishop Wordsworth, at Tisbury Parish Church, 1900s. Back row, left to right: Gertie Penny, Amy Furnall, K. Randall, N. Gauler, Miss Cuff, I. and D. Northover, Miss Read, Miss Russell, H. Penny, N. and K. Kendall. Second row: John Freeman (headmaster), Mr Ford, Mr Howell, Mr Hoare, Mr Clarke, Rev. Ridges, Rev. F.E. Hutchinson, Bishop John Wordsworth (Bishop of Salisbury), Fred Woods, Rev. C. A. Hutchinson, Tom Gauler, Percy Howell, Mr Gatehouse. Third row: Leonard Lane, R. Collins, A. Soper, H. Stevens, Jim Turner, E. Lane, F. and S. Northover. Front row: Sydney Northover, A. Pomeroy, A. Mould, S. Potter, W. Kendall, W. Alford, J. Wilkins, L. Meade, E. Howell, J. Turner, R. Soper, G. Penny. (Tisbury Archives – Miss A. Alford)

Jabez Penny, the road foreman of Tisbury Rural District Council. He was also a local Methodist preacher, still active in the 1930s. (Fred Peckham)

Pictured in Tisbury High Street, 1925, these prize cattle have arrived from Salisbury Market, ready for slaughter. The prominent figures in front are: Jim Cull, Roy Green, Arthur Blandford, Gil Baker (the butcher), Toby Baker (his son) and W. Lloyd. (Toby Baker)

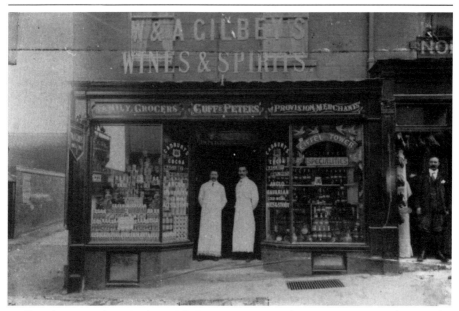

Guff and Peters' shop in the High Street, *c.* 1907. The owners are standing in the doorway, while Dick Northover, draper and clothier, stands to the right. (Tisbury Archives – Miss A. Alford)

Hibberds Ltd, Tisbury's large emporium in the High Street, *c.* 1907. It supplied a remarkable range of products to the surrounding rural area. (Kathleen Mould)

This is believed to be the Peace Carnival, 1918. In the distance is Chantry Hill. (Joyce Jenkyns)

James Street and his daughter, Doris (the late Mrs Tom Genge) at Walmead Farm, 1905. (Daisy Shallcross)

J. Alford's steam engine and thresher outside Place Farm, *c.* 1910. Mr Alford was from Withyslade Farm in Tisbury Row. The drivers are Mr Pullman, Mr Hansford (from The Royal Oak at Swallowcliffe) and a friend. (Tisbury Archives – Miss A. Alford)

Clock House, built by the clock- and watch-maker, Thomas Osmond, whose initials are engraved on the entrance, together with the date 1828. George, his youngest brother, is seen in front. (Toby Baker)

James Ball, master plasterer, purchased Clock House, most probably from the Osmonds, at the end of the 19th century. The Ball family are pictured, left to right: Ben, James, Kathleen, Ethel, Ernest, Lawrence, Jessica, Anna (James' wife). (Toby Baker)

Schoolchildren at Chicksgrove, *c.* 1900. The Rev. F.E. Hutchinson built a school at the little hamlet with a grant from the National Society in 1872. The schoolmistress on the left was probably Florence Orford. (Margaret Mullins)

A class from Tisbury National School, seen here with Mr John Freeman, headmaster from 1904 to 1931. (Tisbury Archives – Miss A. Alford)

The Peace Carnival, 1918. (Kathleen Mould)

Old Stubbles Bridge, 1905. (Tisbury Archives – the late Mrs A. Galpin)

Tisbury 'Town' Band early this century. Edwin Rixon, the stone mason and diarist, is second from left in the front row. (Robert Hardy)

Cyril Cully with his bus and Nadder Valley customers, *c.* 1922. Notice the solid tyres and the maximum speed of 12 mph recorded on the side of the vehicle. (Joyce Jenkyns)

A charabanc outing to Cheddar Caves, early 1930s. Customers include Yvonne Burt, Margery, Mariah and Lawrence Ball and Jessie Lacey. (Toby Baker)

A drawing discovered on the walls of Tisbury Workhouse on Monmouth Hill during its demolition in 1967. (Joyce Jenkyns)

A view of the workhouse at Monmouth Hill, taken through decorative windows during its demolition. Some of these windows were salvaged and can still be seen around the village, notably at Jay's Cottage and at the brewery. (Joyce Jenkyns)

James Rixon (1837–1912) was a stonemason from Zion Hill Cottage. His quaintly carved stone heads – said to represent local characters – can still be seen in walls and gardens in the area. (Doris Hill)

One of James Rixon's carved heads at Duck Street Farm. (Joyce Jenkyns)

A Red Cross detachment was founded in 1914 by Mrs Walter Shaw-Stewart of Fonthill Abbey in a hut in Hindon Lane. During the years 1915–18 the detachment staffed a military hospital at Tisbury Vicarage. The photograph includes Miss Mary Shaw-Stewart (fourth from left, back row), Mrs Walter Shaw-Stewart (fourth from left in the middle), Mrs Edward Young from Arundell House (dark uniform) and Mrs Selina Dogrell from Wallmead Farm on her left. Seated in front on the left is Miss Irene Shaw-Stewart. (Tisbury Archives – Miss A. Alford)

Nurses and patients at Tisbury Vicarage Hospital, 1917. (Joyce Jenkyns)

An early aeroplane at Haygrove (now part of Wallmead Farm), c. 1925. In the cockpit is Gil Baker, the butcher. A ride cost 5s. (Toby Baker)

The tithe barn at Place Farm. Reputedly the biggest in England, it was once the property of the Abbesses of Shaftesbury. (Joyce Jenkyns)

Tisbury Brewery. It was built by Archibald Beckett from Hindon (and rebuilt after a fire in 1885) on the site of the old workhouse. Since then it has served many purposes apart from the brewing of beer, including printing. (Joyce Jenkyns)

Workmen on the steps of Pyt House, the estate of Capt. Jack Benett, *c.* 1930. Back row, left to right: B. Marshalsea, T. Batten, A. Underwood, A. Stafford, W. Loaring, T. Griffiths, D. Parham, A. Kellow. Fourth row, left to right: ? Cox, W. Jinks, N. Mulley, S. Castle, B. Ravenhill, J. Sanger, F. Gane, L. Ranger, K. Mercer, ? Gale, R. Gale. Third row, left to right: ? Trussler, H. Lawrence, G. Garrett, ? Chalk, ? Dicker, F. Sanger, W. Turner, R. Sanger, L. Bone, J. Yeates, W. Sanger. Second row, left to right: W. Penny, T. Loaring, F. Knight, J. Knight, C. Gane, H. Gray, B. Chalke, ? Sanger, P. Read, M. Penny, H. Butt, W. Alford. Front row, left to right: B. Gurd, S. Chapman, ? Sanger, H. Martin, J. Day, S. Culley, B. Gray, P. Lever, W. Coombes, D. Kent, W. Mould, R. Chapman. Absent from this group is Jack Benett's chauffeur, Edgar Stone, who was on his employer's yacht at the time. However, his daughter, Monica Stone, points out that he was 'working – not holidaying!'. (Monica Stone)

SECTION SIX

Chilmark

Beckett's Lane, Chilmark, looking towards the parish church, 1910. (Brenda Hobbs)

The 'Cross', or crossroads, at Chilmark. The building on the left was once the Red Lion Inn. (Peter Simonds)

The Old Rectory in The Street. On the left is the downstairs window under which the skeleton of a girl was allegedly discovered during drainage repairs in the 1890s. (Mary Hare)

Harry Jukes stands outside the Black Dog, early 1930s. He was the landlord from 1892 to 1942. (Peter Simmonds)

Edwin Rixon, one of generations of stonemasons to work in the Chilmark and Tisbury quarries. He lived in at least two cottages at Chilmark early this century and his diaries, from 1904 until his death in 1952, give an interesting picture of rural life in the first half of the 20th century. (Barbara McCoy)

The Blackstone crude-oil engine replaced an earlier steam one in the 1920s. It was used for hauling stone from the stone face to the bottom of the shaft. (Joyce Jenkyns)

Chilmark Quarry, where a large block of stone is being winched on to a trolley. Rixon notes many accidents to the men, who worked in poor conditions and received no compensation for injuries. (Joyce Jenkyns)

The Viney bus ran from Chilmark to Salisbury from 1917. Fred, the driver (far right), lost his leg in a rock fall at the quarry. His brother, Reg (seated at the front of the bus), was the conductor. He had lost an arm as a child. (Mrs Winnie Viney, Fred's widow)

A lunch break for the farm workers at Ridge Farm, *c.* 1925. From left to right: Edward Dennis, Ted Yeates (standing), ? Roud, Charlie Moore, Cyril Snook, Fred Lever, Ern Deverell. (Fred Dennis)

SECTION SEVEN
The Teffonts

Teffont Lodge. Robert Lee brought up his family here when he came to Teffont Manor as coachman (later chauffeur) to Charles Maudslay. The Lodge stands on the junction of the B3089 Barford–Hindon road and the Tisbury road, but here, before the First World War, the Tisbury road was still gated. (Alice Lee)

The road through Teffont Magna, 1930s. Hope Cottage is on the left. (Charlie Merrifield)

A combine harvester, reputedly the first to be used in England, at Manor Farm, Teffont Magna, 1934. It came from the International Harvester Company of America. Jim Brockway is the tractor driver and Bill Crouch, the farmer, is at the controls. Charlie Merrifield is one of the two boys at the back; the other is John Read, the farmer's nephew. (Charlie Merrifield)

The hunt outside the Black Horse at Teffont Magna, mid-1930s. Lucy Lee, one of Robert Lee's daughters, is on the right selling poppies for Armistice Day. (Alice Lee)

William Thomas Brooks' General Stores, opposite the Black Horse, 1905. The sign reads 'Cash Draper and Grocer, Boot and Shoe Stores'. Mr Brooks was formerly a shoemaker at Dinton and his wife, Catherine Jane, ran the post office at Teffont. (Charlie Merrifield)

Visiting the smithy – a pastoral scene at Teffont Evias, just after the Second World War. Ralph Stevens is leading the horses to be shod by the blacksmith, Harry Bull, whose shop lay on the road from Teffont Magna to Evias. (Charlie Merrifield)

Carters Lane, Teffont Evias, early 1900s. It is still possible to see the bricked-up lime kilns, once fed from the stone quarry above and which had formed part of the village economy. (Charlie Merrifield)

Fitz Farmhouse (now The Thatchers). Photographed in the mid-20th century, it was the home of Charlie Giles, after whom the present Farmer Giles' farmstead is named. (John Vining)

Rawlings' bus from Hindon takes a party from the Teffonts on a trip to Bournemouth, 1925. Harry Bull, the blacksmith, can be seen in the centre carrying his young son. His wife is to his left and his daughter, Nellie, is on his right (in a white bonnet). (Alice Lee)

Charles Maudslay stands with his sister Isobel outside the entrance of Teffont Manor, 1900s. (Alice Lee)

Fitz Farm, next to Fitz House. It was bought by Charlie Giles as a sitting tenant in 1951 when the estate was sold. The land now forms part of the Farmer Giles' Leisure Complex and the buildings have recently been replaced by a private residence. (Charlie Merrifield)

Dinton

Charles Gerry's Bakery and Stores, 1920s. Rebuilt by Lord Pembroke from old farm cottages in 1902, the shop has maintained its central position at the bottom of Snowhill since the 19th century. The old post office on the left was demolished to straighten the road in the 1950s. (Dinton WI Scrapbook, 1956)

The Wyndham Arms' Slate Club, 1910. (Dinton WI Scrapbook)

Dinton Band, which was formed in 1900. The photograph includes B. Whatley, A. Dyer, H. Shepard, G. Burt, Tom Davis, E. Shute, W. Baker and J. Scammell. (Dinton WI Scrapbook)

Marshwood was originally a keeper's cottage. It was greatly enlarged by the addition of a wing at each end to accommodate the Wyndham family during the building of the new Dinton House (now Philipps House), which was completed in 1815. (Dinton WI Scrapbook)

Mr Darling poses in front of his home at Marshwood, 1900. He had arrived from Scotland in the 1840s to work on the Wyndham Estate, as bailiff and steward of Dinton House. At first he caused great mirth with his Scottish attire, as the villagers had never seen a kilt! (Dinton WI Scrapbook)

Dinton brick workers, *c*. 1927. (Dinton WI Scrapbook)

The Clark family. Jim Clark and his wife Helena (née Cockeain) are pictured on their wedding day, 24 July 1916, prior to his departure for India with the Wiltshire Regiment. Behind are Jim's four brothers and their wives. The only member of the family still in Dinton is Jim's son, Ewart, who runs a market-garden business. (Alice Lee)

These First World War soldiers are believed to have been photographed at Dinton. Standing in the centre is William George 'Nimble' Wilton, who married Elsie Wyatt of Dinton post office. William was born in 1898 and enlisted in the Wiltshire Regiment on 3 June 1916. (Alan Clayton)

Miss Constance Penruddocke, 'Miss Penn', was the sister of Charles Penruddocke of Compton Park. She lived at Cotterells in Snowhill and was much respected for her hospitality to First World War troops – especially Australians. (Dinton WI Scrapbook)

Vivian Townsend was gamekeeper to Bertram Erasmus Philipps of Dinton House (now known as Philipps House) from 1916 to 1940. Also pictured is his wife Ellen (left), his daughter Margaret and Raymond, his grandson by another daughter, Gladys. (Dinton WI Scrapbook)

Dinton station, 1905. Situated on the Waterloo–Exeter line, it was eventually closed in 1966. (Dinton WI Scrapbook)

Snowhill, early 1900s. According to Lou Winter's *Tales of a Carter's Daughter*, these thatched cottages (now demolished) were known as Oborne Cottages and Snowhill Cottage. (Alan Clayton)

Members of the Dinton Methodist Chapel, *c.* 1931. (Alan Clayton)

William Wyatt (1871–1938) was Grand Master of the Oddfellows Lodge, Dinton. He was also the church organist at Compton Chamberlayne, his birthplace, and later at Baverstock. There he also conducted the Dinton Choral Society and hand-bell ringers, and was captain of the bell ringers. He was a practised thatcher and was Dinton's sub-postmaster for thirty-three years until 1938. (Alan Clayton)

The post office at Dinton, now demolished. John and Elsie, son and daughter of William Wyatt, stand outside. Elsie later married William 'Nimble' Wilton and was a teacher at Dinton School. The dog's name was Spider! (Alan Clayton)

Dinton School, *c*. 1904. (Dinton WI Scrapbook)

A gathering of schoolchildren at Dinton (now Philipps) House, 1920. (Dinton WI Scrapbook)

A Sunday School group pictured outside the old school attached to Hyde House (now a National Trust property) in 1929. (Dinton WI Scrapbook)

Reg Baker, the Dinton blacksmith, photographed just after the Second World War. His forge, on the corner of Spracklands, has recently been replaced by houses. (Dinton WI Scrapbook)

Getting the metal tyre out of oven.

Putting tyre on wheel.

Cooling.

Wheel finished.

The wheelwright, Walter Clark, is seen at work, 1954. Assisting him are Cyril Lever and Reg Baker, the blacksmith. Because of the mechanisation of agricultural machinery, wheels of this kind are now very rarely required. (Dinton WI Scrapbook)

An immaculately turned-out company of American servicemen, stationed at the new depot at Dinton during the Second World War. The hangars can still be seen behind houses and form part of RAF Chilmark, which is to be closed in 1995. The depot was built to supply the American Army and Air Force with equipment for D-Day. (Alan Clayton)

Residents moving from the old American Air Force Nissen huts, c. 1945. These had provided homes for young couples from the village who were unable to find accommodation after the Second World War. Pictured from left to right: Mrs Kelly and daughter (Ben Clayton is behind), Jim Gipson and daughter, Mrs Scammell and daughter, Sam Randall. (Gladys Gipson)

SECTION NINE

Barford St Martin and Burcombe

The village street at Barford St Martin, before the First World War. The post office is to the far right and the church is in the distance. (Barford and Burcombe WI Scrapbook, 1956)

Gaul Bridge, Barford St Martin, crosses the Nadder, and is now part of the main A30 road. The young man seen here is Jesse Avery, who was born in 1893 and lived nearby at Four Winds. (Robert Chalke)

Barford Cross stands outside the church. Its age is uncertain but it is believed to be older than the church itself, possibly having replaced a wooden cross used by early missionaries as a preaching station. (Barford and Burcombe WI Scrapbook)

Shire horses at Barford St Martin, *c*. 1918. From left to right, Fred Miles, Fred Penny and Frank Daniels are the carters. (Barford and Burcombe WI Scrapbook)

The Green Dragon at Barford decorated for Edward VIII's coronation, 1936. The landlord, Ernest Harvey, is standing outside. (Robert Chalke)

Thomas Dawkins, *c.* 1904. His family were builders in Barford St Martin and donated the stained-glass windows in the chancel of the church. (Robert Chalke)

An unknown inhabitant of Barford St Martin, photographed at the beginning of the century. (Barford and Burcombe WI Scrapbook)

Barford St Martin School group, 1904. The headmaster is Frank Foster and his wife Harriet, the junior teacher, is shown on the right. Also included are their daughter, Dorothy (standing in the centre), Edgar Whatley, Reg Dawkins, Edward Rampton, and Edith and Dorothy Chalke.

Burcombe School, c. 1918. Alfred Gumbleton, son of the landlord of the Ship Inn, is seated on the far right. He later worked as a telegraph boy at Wilton but died at the age of seventeen. (Violet Cheverell)

A charabanc outing from Burcombe, probably to Weymouth, *c.* 1920. The Sparrow and Vincent bus is from Salisbury. Vi Cheverell and her mother, Jane, from the Ship Inn, are at the back (centre). Vi recalls that 'the children were always given a bag of gooseberries to eat and a streamer to throw from the bus!' (Violet Cheverell)

The Barford and Burcombe WI outing to the Isle of Wight, 1955. (Barford and Burcombe WI Scrapbook)

Hurdcott House, early this century. During the First World War, Hurdcott House became the headquarters of No. 3 Command Depot of the Australian Imperial Force. Many sick and wounded returned there from the front. The hamlet of Hurdcott has until recently been part of the parish of Baverstock, but was united with Barford in 1884. (Barford and Burcombe WI Scrapbook)

Grovely Lodge in Grovely Wood, early this century. Today, this is all that remains of a village that, before the Second World War, boasted a church and a school. (Barford and Burcombe WI Scrapbook)

A view of the Nadder at Burcombe, between the wars. (Barford and Burcombe WI
Scrapbook)

Burcombe Manor was built in the mid-19th century, reputedly to house Lord Herbert of
Lea, the friend and supporter of Florence Nightingale. (Barford and Burcombe WI
Scrapbook)

SECTION TEN

Ansty and Swallowcliffe

The Commandery at Ansty is thought to have been the first riding school in the country. It was probably built on the site of a hospice used for the care of travellers and the sick by the Knights Hospitallers of St John, in the 13th century. (Tony Keating)

Ansty House, opposite the pond. In the 19th and early 20th century it was the home of the Lever family who were builders, carpenters and wheelwrights. All the workshops (notice the clock and bell) were removed in the early 1950s; only the house remains. (Joan Parsons)

Charles Edgar Lever (left) sits in a milk cart outside his home, Ansty House, 1920s. (Joan Parsons)

Ansty Band, *c.* 1925. Back row, left to right: Harry Feltham, Joe Lever, Steve Parsons, Louis Macey, Fred Parsons, Fred Gurd, William Rixon, William Parsons, Steve Parsons (from Salisbury), Charles Feltham. Front row, left to right: Alf Jay, Alf Yeates, John Parsons, Joe Lever (from Wardour), Charles Lever (from Wardour), Nobby Lever. The Parsons and Feltham families are still represented in the village. (Joan Parsons and Jack Feltham)

A coach party from Ansty, including the band, are pictured in New Canal, Salisbury, 1925. (Jack Feltham)

The Arundell Arms (now the Maypole Inn), 1903. The licensee at that time was Walter Gray. Notice that one bicycle seen here (left) has pneumatic tyres while the other has solid tyres. Dunlop first made pneumatic tyres successfully in 1890. (Brian Hamshere, the Maypole Inn)

An outing from Ansty, c. 1935. This group includes most of 'the fighting Sullivans' – five of the six daughters and the three sons, who served in the ATS and the army during the Second World War. From left to right: Ken Parsons, Ivy Sullivan, Phyllis Sullivan, Mrs Main, Millicent Sullivan, Ruth Sullivan, Mrs Mounty, -?-, Mrs Sullivan, -?-, -?-, Isabel Parsons, Ron Parsons, Rosie Mullins, Maud Parsons, -?-, Mollie Sullivan, Mrs Mullins, -?-. (Joan Parsons)

Haymaking at Frog Pond Farm, 1920s. Many of the villagers turned out to help. Charles Edgar Lever is seen holding the horse (left); Herbie Lever is behind him with the rake; George Parsons, the dairy farmer from Lower Farm, stands with his milk cart (right). George also made the village supply of cider! (Joan Parsons)

George William Parsons and his wife, Annie Lever Parsons, in 1933 with their children, Ron (standing, left), Joan, who died aged ten, Isabelle and Kenneth. They were tenants at Lower Farm. The Parsons were Roman Catholic tenants on the Wardour estate for about five generations. Ron later worked for Doug Davis at the Manor Farm from around 1943 to 1957 and then took over the tenancy of the Arundell Arms. Annie played the organ at Ansty Church, while the rest of her family attended the small RC chapel in the village. (Joan Parsons)

An outing from Swallowcliffe School to see the *Queen Mary* at Southampton Docks, *c.* 1935. The party included Winnie Hutchinson, Joyce Hoskins, Ena Feltham, Margaret Beale, Charles Brown, William Rixon, Percy Hutchinson, James Gray, Douglas Rixon, Maurice Rixon, Olive Hoskins, Beryl Bugden, Daisy Stainer, Ernie Hutchinson, Ronald Parsons, J. Parsons, F.E. Cross, H. Townson, R. Hoskins, E.D. Hoskins, A.L. Hoskins, A.L. Parsons, A.M. Cole, G.C. Townson, Jack Harris, Joe Harris, Gordon Hoskins and Wilfred Hoskins. The teacher at the back (third from left) was Flo Cross. (Joan Parsons)

A view of Swallowcliffe, with St Peter's Church in the distance, around the time of the First World War. (Mrs S. Jenkins)

St Peter's Church, Swallowcliffe, early this century. The manor house can be seen in the background. (Mrs S. Jenkins)

A row of cottages in front of Swallowcliffe Church. Although these were demolished in the 1950s, a vestige of them remains in the church wall. (Marion Andrews)

Thomas Edwin Wright, the wheelwright and carpenter, is pictured with his wife Sarah (née Foote) and children at Vine Cottage, Swallowcliffe, early this century. (Mrs S. Jenkins)

Swallowcliffe village shop, seen here in the early years of this century, was run by Thomas Spencer, grocer and linen-draper. He was helped by his wife and six daughters. The girl on the right is Ethel Turner. (Mrs S. Jenkins)

Springhead Cottages, Swallowcliffe, were built on the Alfords' land. The family were well-known local farmers, and their manor house is visible in the distance. (Mrs S. Jenkins)

An illuminated address, presented by the villagers of Swallowcliffe to the farmer, William Keevil, on his retirement in 1907. At the top is a drawing of the manor house, before the present northern wing was added. (Gill and Tony Rose)

THE MANOR, SWALLOWCLIFFE, NEAR TISBURY, WILTS

Swallowcliffe Manor is the oldest building in the village. To the right is the north wing, which was rebuilt, probably in the early 1920s, by Capt. Henry Cavendish, a cousin of the Duke of Devonshire. (Ray Tuffin)

The old post office at Swallowcliffe, 1906. The last postmistress when it closed by 1931 was Mary 'Polly' Burt. Situated on the main A30 road, it has become a picturesque private dwelling. (Mrs S. Jenkins)

Sutton Mandeville

The Cribbage Hut, late 1920s. Situated on the A30, it was demolished when the new Cribbage Hut (now the Lancers) was built further to the east in 1935. The landlord, Albert Trulock Spenser, son of the miller at Sutton Mandeville, is seen standing with his wife and their poodle. With them is Harry Hardiman, licensee of the Compasses at Chicksgrove. (Gill and Tony Rose)

William Wyndham (seated) with his son, from Dinton House. The Wyndham estates included Dinton, Sutton Mandeville and Chicksgrove from the late 17th until the early 20th century. The eldest son of each generation was always called William. (Margaret Mullins)

Bailey Hill Farmhouse, Sutton Row, 1920s. Sarah Gray, widow of the farmer, Benedict Gray, is seen with her son, Cyril, who supplemented the family income by running the first bus in the area, an old Ford T model. (Ron Gray)

This group is celebrating Queen Victoria's Diamond Jubilee at Sutton Mandeville, 1897.
(Margaret Mullins)

Sheep shearing in the barn of Manor Farm. This was taken during the time of William Miles. Kelly's Directory shows him to have been farmer and miller in the village in the 1880s. His widow, Eliza, was still farming there in the 1930s. (Les Feltham)

Employees on Manor Farm, May 1923. They include M. Thick, J. Hardiman, F. Cross, Alf Mullins, W. and F. Thick, H. Johnson, B. Gunston and C. Cannon. (Margaret Mullins)

The schoolhouse, *c*. 1900. Miss Elizabeth Roper and Bessie Cross are the teachers. (Margaret Mullins)

Sutton Mandeville School, *c*. 1935. The group includes Fred Spenser, the miller's grandson (left, back row); Margaret Mullins (fifth from left, back row); Ron Gray (seated, front left). Mrs Kill (left) and Miss Brown (right) are the teachers. (Margaret Mullins)

Ivy Cottage (now known as Bonds),
c. 1905. Margaret and Frank
Mullins were smallholders here,
with a family of fourteen children.
(Margaret Mullins)

Frank Mullins is pictured with the two Miss Bakers, Miss Coombes and Jack the
donkey, before the First World War. (Margaret Mullins)

Frank Mullins jr (left) is seen cutting the Rectory Field with Jim Dean, between the wars. Frank had recently retired from his butcher's shop in Salisbury. (Margaret Mullins)

Frank Mullins sr (centre, by the door) retired to Glasses Hill Cottage. Also seen here, in 1929, is his only daughter, Dorothy, and her four-year-old niece, Margaret, who still lives here today. Gilbert Mullins, one of Frank's thirteen sons, is to the right. He was a gardener in the village. (Margaret Mullins)

The Rev. William Louis Walter was the much-loved vicar at Sutton Mandeville between the wars. His wife is on the right. (Margaret Mullins)

This sweet and tobacco shop is in a house in Sutton Road, now known as The Stables. Established before the First World War, the shop was in the right-hand part of the house and was kept by another of the Mullins family – Alfred. (Margaret Mullins)

SECTION TWELVE

Fovant and Compton Chamberlayne

Fovant High Street, 1900s. The Crosskeys Inn, on the A30, can be seen in the distance.
(Roy Nuttall)

Fovant is situate in the midst of a district noted for its ancient earthworks, and many Roman coins have been found in quarries near, which proves that the quarries are of very great antiquity.

Another view of Fovant High Street, with the London City & Midland Bank in the foreground. This picture dates from the First World War. (Roy Nuttall)

Albert Jukes, photographed outside his shop, before the First World War. Kelly's Directory for 1907 indicates that he also ran the stores at nearby Compton Chamberlayne. The Crosskeys Inn is in the distance. (Roy Nuttall)

The National Stores, Fovant, during the First World War. The proprietor was John White. (Roy Nuttall)

Fovant Band gather outside the Pembroke Arms on the Slate Club Feast Day, 1900s. The Feast Day was last held in 1911. The stables seen here in the background have been replaced by a car park. (Roy Nuttall)

Carpenters at Fovant Camp during the First World War. The photograph includes (back row): Had Chalke, Harry Dawkins, Edward 'Sonny' Rampton and Reg Dawkins. (Robert Chalke)

Walter and Florence Mullins, pictured outside the Crosskeys Inn on their wedding day, 1907. They were to take over the inn in the late 1920s after the death of Elizabeth and Edwin Perrett, Florence's parents. They remained there until 1942, when they both died. (Olive Mullins)

'The Little Grey Home' was a thatched garden-house at Cotterells, Dinton. This was the home of Miss Constance Penruddocke, who, like many others in the Nadder Valley, entertained troops from army camps in the Fovant area during the First World War. (Dinton WI Scrapbook)

Charles Mason, the carpenter, works on the coffer and screen for Fovant Church, *c.* 1933, using wood from Hyde's Copse, Dinton. (Dinton WI Scrapbook)

A road maintenance gang at Fovant, early 1920s. Peter Daniels believes these steam road-rollers were made by Aveling (left) and Marshall (right). Fred Mullins is second from the left. (Peter Daniels)

The lodge gatehouse to Compton House, Compton Chamberlayne, situated on the A30. The gatehouse remained a residence until the 1960s but this photograph was probably taken before the First World War. (John Newman)

Compton House, Compton Chamberlayne. Built in Tudor Gothic style in 1550 by Sir Edward Penruddocke, it was later remodelled in the early Stuart style and remained with the family until 1930. St Michael's Church lies behind. (John Newman)

A service of dedication of the Australian flag outside St Michael's Church, 1951. The flag was to be placed on the map of Australia, carved on Compton Down by Australian troops during the First World War. The flagholder is Mr Dyer of Fovant Home Guard. Also shown are the Rev. Mr Bazelgette, vicar of Compton Chamberlayne, an Australian soldier and Willie Langdon. (Willie Langdon)

The flag is raised on the map of Australia. (Willie Langdon)

This photograph shows the extended family of John Wyatt, hurdle-, spar- and gad-maker, assembled in the orchard of their cottage, 1900s. The photograph includes (back row) William Wyman, Jack Trent, Bill Fry; (second row) Elsie Pringle (later Wilton), William Wyatt, Dora Pringle (later Adams), Frances Emma Wyatt (née Pringle), Olive May Wyatt (later Trent); (third row) Ethel Wyman with baby George, John and Sarah Wyatt; (children seated) Frances Wyatt (later Clayton), John Wyatt, William Wyatt, James Wyatt, Gladys Nevell (later Scammell), Florence Jane Wyatt (later Hallett). (Arthur Trent)

William and Frances Wyatt and their family, who left Compton Chamberlayne in 1905, when William became sub-postmaster at Dinton (*see* p. 80). They are pictured at the home of his father, John Wyatt, the spar- and hurdle-maker. Back row, left to right: Elsie, Dora, Jim. Front row, left to right: Frances, William, Billy, Frances (née Pringle), Jack, Florrie. (Alan Clayton)

William Langdon, the farmer from Manor Farm, Compton Chamberlayne, *c*. 1900. (Willie Langdon)

SECTION THIRTEEN

Wilton

The Market Cross and the ruins of St Mary's Church, at the turn of the century. The Cross was restored by Nancy Morland when she was Mayor of Wilton, 1990–91. (Nancy Morland)

Floods at Waterditchampton, Wilton, 1910. This photograph was taken from the railway bridge. (Nancy Morland)

West Street, *c*. 1919. The stationery shop of Mr W. Boning, who produced many early postcards of Wilton, is on the left. The saddler's shop is next door. (Nancy Morland)

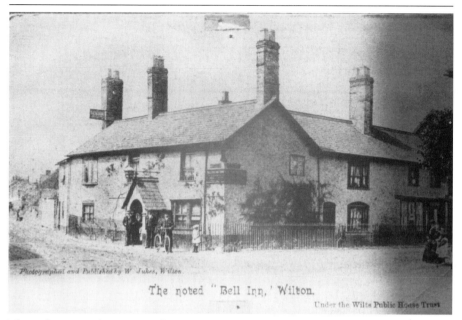

The Bell Inn on the corner of West Street and the Ditchampton road, 1900s. (Nancy Morland)

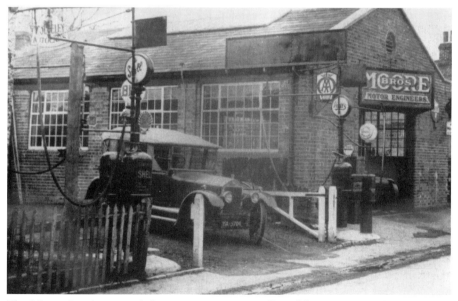

The Moore Brothers' workshops, *c.* 1924. Originally a filling-station and car-stockist, the firm could not obtain a franchise for petrol during the Second World War when it was rationed. They therefore converted their business to the reconditioning of engines. (Nancy Morland)

The home of William Vincent Moore jr, his wife, Agnes and their ten children. William was the owner of the scrap-merchant business in West Street. The house is seen here decorated for the coronation of George V in 1910. It stands on the corner of Crow Lane and West Street and is now three separate shops. (Nancy Morland)

Workers at Wilton Felt Mill (now Naish Felts Ltd), late 1930s. Centre, with cap, is 'Tip' Turner, the foreman, who was very much in charge. Also included are Reg Brown, Harry Dewland, Reg Sainsbury, Charlie Dawkins, Mr Simmonds and Mr Canning snr. (John Naish)

North Street, before the First World War. The house on the right, which is possibly of Tudor origin or earlier, is one of the oldest in Wilton. It belonged to the Wilton Educational Charities and is now a private house. (Nancy Morland)

Crowds celebrate the coronation of George V, 22 June 1911, on what was obviously a wet day. (Nancy Morland)

Workers at the Wilton Royal Carpet Factory, just after the Second World War. The firm stopped producing hand-made Axminster and Wilton carpets in 1956, when production became fully mechanised. (Chris Rousell)

Acknowledgements

The enjoyment I obtained from the compilation of this book lies as much in the number of friends I made as in the photographs I acquired. These I have acknowledged in my introduction. More specifically I should like to thank the individuals and organisations whose photographs appear in this book:

Miss A. Alford • Marion Andrews • Toby Baker
Barford and Burcombe WI Scrapbook • Pamela Bown • Robert Chalke
Violet Cheverell • Alan Clayton • Peter Daniels • Fred Dennis
Dinton WI Scrapbook • The Donheads WI Scrapbook • Jack Feltham
Les Feltham • The Fonthills WI Scrapbook • the late Mrs Adeline Galpin
Louisa George • Gladys Gipson • Ron Gray • Brian Hamshere
Muriel Harding • Robert Hardy • Mary Hare • Reg Harris • Vi Head
Doris Hill • Hindon Village Hall Archives • Brenda Hobbs • Mrs S. Jenkins
Joyce Jenkyns • Joyce Johnson • Tony Keating • Willie Langdon • Alice Lee
Barbara McCoy • Charlie Merrifield • Nancy Morland • Kathleen Mould
Margaret Mullins • Olive Mullins • John Naish • John Newman • Roy Nuttall
• Joan Parsons • Fred Peckham • Agnes Penny • David Ricketts
Gill and Tony Rose • Chris Rousell • Semley WI Scrapbook • Daisy Shallcross
• Peter Simmonds • Monica Stone • The Tisbury Archives • Arthur Trent
Ray Tuffin • Winnie Viney • John Vining • G.P. Wencki